A Man's Strategy for Conquering Temptation

Bob Vereen

PRECEPT MINISTRIES INTERNATIONAL

WATERBROOK
PRESS

A Man's Strategy for Conquering Temptation
Published by WaterBrook Press
12265 Oracle Boulevard, Suite 200
Colorado Springs, Colorado 80921

All Scripture quotations, unless otherwise indicated, are taken from the New American Standard Bible® (NASB). © Copyright The Lockman Foundation 1960, 1962, 1963, 1968, 1971, 1972, 1973, 1975, 1977, 1995. Used by permission. (www.Lockman.org).

Italics in Scripture quotations reflect the author's added emphasis.

ISBN 978-0-307-45761-5

Previously published under the title *How Can a Man Control His Thoughts, Desires, and Passions?*

Published in the United States by WaterBrook Multnomah, an imprint of the Crown Publishing Group, a division of Random House Inc., New York.

WATERBROOK and its deer colophon are registered trademarks of Random House Inc.

Printed in the United States of America
2009

10 9 8 7 6 5 4 3 2 1

SPECIAL SALES
Most WaterBrook Multnomah books are available at special quantity discounts when purchased in bulk by corporations, organizations, and special-interest groups. Custom imprinting or excerpting can also be done to fit special needs. For information, please e-mail SpecialMarkets@WaterBrookMultnomah.com or call 1-800-603-7051.

HOW TO USE THIS STUDY

This small-group study is for people who are interested in learning for themselves more about what the Bible says on various subjects, but who have only limited time to meet together. It's ideal, for example, for a lunch group at work, an early morning men's group, a young mothers' group meeting in a home, a Sunday-school class, or even family devotions. (It's also ideal for small groups that typically have longer meeting times—such as evening groups or Saturday morning groups—but want to devote only a portion of their time together to actual study, while reserving the rest for prayer, fellowship, or other activities.)

This book is designed so that all the group's participants will complete each lesson's study activities *at the same time.* Discussing your insights drawn from what God says about the subject reveals exciting, life-impacting truths.

Although it's a group study, you'll need a facilitator to lead the study and keep the discussion moving. (This person's function is *not* that of a lecturer or teacher. However, when this book is used in a Sunday-school class or similar setting, the teacher should feel free to lead more directly and to bring in other insights in addition to those provided in each week's lesson.)

If *you* are your group's facilitator, the leader, here are some helpful points for making your job easier:

- Go through the lesson and mark the text before you lead the group. This will give you increased familiarity with the material and will enable you to facilitate the group with greater ease. It may be easier for you to lead the group through the instructions for marking if you, as a leader, choose a specific color for each symbol you mark.

- As you lead the group, start at the beginning of the text and simply read it aloud in the order it appears in the lesson, including the "insight boxes," which appear throughout. Work through the lesson together, observing and discussing what you learn. As you read the Scripture verses, have the group say aloud the word they are marking in the text.

- The discussion questions are there simply to help you cover the material. As the class moves into the discussion, many times you will find that they will cover the questions on their own. Remember, the discussion questions are there to guide the group through the topic, not to squelch discussion.

- Remember how important it is for people to verbalize their answers and discoveries. This greatly strengthens their personal understanding of each week's lesson. Try to ensure that everyone has plenty of opportunity to contribute to each week's discussions.

- Keep the discussion moving. This may mean spending more time on some parts of the study than on others. If necessary, you should feel free to spread out a lesson over more than one session. However, remember that you don't want to slow the pace too much. It's much better to leave everyone "wanting more" than to have people dropping out because of declining interest.

- If the validity or accuracy of some of the answers seems questionable, you can gently and cheerfully remind the group to stay focused on the truth of the Scriptures. Your object is to learn what the Bible says, not to engage in human philosophy. Simply stick with the Scriptures and give God the opportunity to speak. His Word *is* truth (John 17:17)!

A MAN'S STRATEGY FOR CONQUERING TEMPTATION

We live in a visual world. Every marketer knows that capturing the attention of a potential client is crucial, and visual appeal is key to stimulating a positive first impression. This is one of the reasons we see so much seductive sexual imagery in advertising and marketing. Every merchandiser around the world knows that he can capture the attention of most men through sexually explicit images. Every male product imaginable is being promoted by an attractive woman in seductive apparel.

We live in a world inundated with sexual images. Some of the most popular television programs among men today are filled with scenes of nudity, passion, and promiscuity. Men are renting pornographic video movies at an alarming rate. Husbands are staying up late, after the wife and kids are in bed, tuning into their favorite late-night porn cable channel or hooking up to one of many pornographic Web sites. *After all,* they tell themselves, *I'm just looking, not touching.*

We live in a promiscuous world. The divorce rate is staggering. Immorality is becoming the norm. Sexual activity outside of marriage is condoned and promoted in every way imaginable. Sexual misconduct is becoming commonplace in even the most sacred of professions.

In the midst of this unbelievable bombardment of sexual immorality, is there any chance that a man can control his thoughts, passions, and desires? Should he even try? What does the Bible say about today's sexual standards? How can a man resist the temptations he faces on a daily basis? How can he overcome his weaknesses? How can he keep his thoughts under control, his passions in check, and his desires in line?

These are just a few of the questions we want to answer as we search the Bible *inductively* regarding this subject. This means you will observe the Word of God for yourself. Once you discover what it says and means, you can then adjust your life to live accordingly.

Let's get started.

Rules for behavior generally are established by the society in which one lives. Sometimes traditional values are written as laws, and sometimes they are simply understood and embraced by the majority of its members. With the passing of time, standards may change for a variety of reasons. What is considered acceptable behavior today may have once been deplored, and what was considered normal behavior at some point in time may one day be labeled "old-fashioned."

God, too, has established rules for behavior. His standard, however, never changes; it has remained the same throughout the ages.

Which standard should the believer follow—God's or the one established by his society? And in what area of life will a man experience the greatest pull between two standards? In what specific ways does God's standard differ from our society's, and how should it impact our daily choices?

Let's see what we can learn about the answers to these questions as we dig into God's Word.

OBSERVE

Leader: Read 1 Thessalonians 4:1-8 aloud.

- *As you read these verses, have the group say aloud and circle every reference to* ***the recipients,*** *particularly the pronouns* ***you, your,*** *and* ***us*** *(when "us" refers to all believers).*

1 THESSALONIANS 4:1-8

1 Finally then, brethren, we request and exhort you in the Lord Jesus, that as you received from us instruction as to how you ought to walk and

please God (just as you actually do walk), that you excel still more.

2 For you know what commandments we gave you by the authority of the Lord Jesus.

3 For this is the will of God, your sanctification; that is, that you abstain from sexual immorality;

4 that each of you know how to possess his own vessel in sanctification and honor,

5 not in lustful passion, like the Gentiles who do not know God;

6 and that no man transgress and defraud his brother in the matter because the Lord is

INSIGHT

The word *walk* in verse 1 describes one's lifestyle, conduct, or behavior.

DISCUSS

• What did you learn from marking the references to the recipients?

• Considering the definition in the Insight box and looking closely at verses 1 and 2, what would following the instructions and commandments enable the recipients to do?

OBSERVE

Leader: *Read aloud 1 Thessalonians 4:1-8 again. This time have the group call out the following key words as they mark them as follows:*

• *Draw a box around each occurrence of the word* **sanctification.**

• *Draw a cloud shape like this* ☁ *around the words* **sexual immorality, lustful passion,** *and* **impurity.**

INSIGHT

The word *sanctification* refers to that ongoing, daily process of becoming holy and pure in mind and body, consecrated to God for His purposes and living separated from the influences of a sinful society.

DISCUSS

• According to verse 3, what is God's will for the believer?

• Look at each place you marked the word *sanctification*. What lifestyle was Paul contrasting with the sanctified lifestyle?

• What did Paul say believers had to "abstain from" in order to be sanctified?

the avenger in all these things, just as we also told you before and solemnly warned you.

7 For God has not called us for the purpose of impurity, but in sanctification.

8 So, he who rejects this is not rejecting man but the God who gives His Holy Spirit to you.

• According to verse 7, for what purpose has God called us?

• If a man ignores Paul's teaching regarding the relationship between sanctification and immorality, whom is he rejecting?

INSIGHT

Sexual immorality refers to any sexual activity outside of the biblical marriage relationship between one man and one woman.

In the Greek the word translated as *abstain* is in the present tense, implying a continuous, habitual, ongoing lifestyle.

Many of the new believers in Thessalonica had formerly participated in pagan religious ceremonies where sexual immorality was part of the worship experience. In addition sexual immorality of all forms was accepted as the norm in their culture.

• Considering the culture in which the Thessalonians lived (see Insight box), why do you think Paul raised the issue of sexual immorality in connection with pleasing God? How might this be a particular concern for this group of believers?

• What similarities, if any, do you see between their culture and ours?

• What are some of the messages our culture sends men today regarding sexual immorality?

OBSERVE

Leader: Read aloud 1 Thessalonians 4:3-5 again.

• *As you read these verses, have the group double underline the word **vessel**.*

1 THESSALONIANS 4:3-5

3 For this is the will of God, your sanctification; that is, that you abstain from sexual immorality;

4 that each of you know how to possess his own vessel in sanctification and honor,

5 not in lustful passion, like the Gentiles who do not know God.

INSIGHT

In verse 4, Paul used the word *vessel* to describe something that the Thessalonian believers were to possess "in sanctification and honor." Theologians are somewhat divided as to whether Paul was referring to one's *body* or one's *wife* when he used the word *vessel*. In the original Greek, the same word carries both definitions in the New Testament. Whatever Paul intended, both interpretations demand that the believer live before God in holiness and purity.

The word *possess* basically means "to get for oneself, purchase, or acquire." It also carries the connotation of having something under control. If his wife is the vessel a man is to "possess," then the believer is to acquire and maintain a marriage relationship that honors God through its sexual purity. If it is his body that a man is to "possess," then he is to keep the desires of his flesh under control at all times and not engage in any sexual activity that is not holy and pure.

DISCUSS

• In light of the context of verses 3-5, if verse 4 read, "that each of you know how to possess his own *body* in sanctification and honor," how would that affect a man's daily choices?

• What boundaries does this set for a man, whether single or married, regarding what he does with his body?

• If verse 4 read, "that each of you know how to possess his own *wife* in sanctification and honor," how would that affect a man's marriage relationship?

• How should this affect what takes place between the husband and wife in the marriage bed? Are all behaviors biblically legitimate, or do the words *sanctification* and *honor* imply some limitations?

• According to this passage, what could prevent you from having the will of God accomplished in your life?

• Based on all you've learned from this passage in 1 Thessalonians, what is God's standard for the believer, and what must the believer do to attain it?

1 PETER 3:7

You husbands in the same way, live with your wives in an understanding way, as with someone weaker, since she is a woman; and show her honor as a fellow heir of the grace of life, so that your prayers will not be hindered.

OBSERVE

Keeping in mind the definition of vessel as wife, let's further consider Paul's instruction to possess one's vessel in sanctification and honor. We'll look at some verses that deal with the man, his wife, the marriage relationship—and how these relate to his sanctification.

Leader: *Read aloud 1 Peter 3:7.*
 • *Have the group underline the words* **wives, she,** *and* **her.**

INSIGHT

The phrase *someone weaker* could be literally translated as "a weaker vessel," using the same word that appears in 1 Thessalonians 4:4.

DISCUSS

• How are wives described in this passage?

• How are they to be treated?

• How does living with your wife "in an understanding way" affect your sexual relationship with your wife?

• If a husband does not show his wife honor, what effect will it have on him?

OBSERVE

Leader: *Read aloud 1 Corinthians 7:2.*
  • *Have the group draw a cloud around the word* **immoralities.**

DISCUSS

• According to this verse, why does a man need his own wife and a woman need her own husband?

1 CORINTHIANS 7:2

But because of immoralities, each man is to have his own wife, and each woman is to have her own husband.

HEBREWS 13:4

Marriage is to be held in honor among all, and the marriage bed is to be undefiled; for fornicators and adulterers God will judge.

OBSERVE

Leader: *Read Hebrews 13:4 aloud.*

> • *Have the group underline each occurrence of the word* **marriage.**

INSIGHT

The word *fornicators* refers to those who engage in sexual immorality, which the Bible defines as the following:

- sex with biological family members or those related by marriage (incest)
- sex with animals (bestiality)
- sex with someone of the same sex (homosexuality and lesbianism)
- any sexual activity with a person to whom you are not married, which includes pedophilia, prostitution, casual sex, etc.

An *adulterer* is a married person who commits a sexual act with someone other than the spouse.

DISCUSS

• What did you learn about marriage from this verse?

• What defiles the marriage bed?

• If the marriage bed is defiled, what will happen to the offender?

• Is viewing sexual images on the Internet, in movies, or in magazines—anything that stimulates the imagination regarding sex with someone who's not your wife—consistent with honoring the marriage bed? Explain your answer.

OBSERVE

Now let's take the definition of vessel as body and examine some verses that deal with the man and his body and how this relates to his sanctification.

Leader: Read 1 Corinthians 6:12-20. Have the group do the following:
  • *Underline each occurrence of the phrase* ***do you not know.***

1 CORINTHIANS 6:12-20

12 All things are lawful for me, but not all things are profitable. All things are lawful for me, but I will not be mastered by anything.

13 Food is for the stomach and the stomach is for food, but God will do away with both of them. Yet the body is not for immorality, but for the Lord, and the Lord is for the body.

14 Now God has not only raised the Lord, but will also raise us up through His power.

15 Do you not know that your bodies are members of Christ? Shall I then take away the members of Christ and make them members of a prostitute? May it never be!

16 Or do you not know that the one who joins himself to a prostitute is one body with her? For He says, "The two shall become one flesh."

- *Draw a box around every mention of **body** or **bodies**.*
- *Draw a cloud around every occurrence of **immorality** or **immoral**.*

DISCUSS

- What did you learn from marking references to the body?

- What happens when a man joins himself to a prostitute?

- What happens when a man joins himself to the Lord?

- How does what we do with our bodies affect our sanctification?

- What liberties do you have with your body?

• According to verse 18, what are we commanded to do? Why?

• From what you read in verse 20, what should be the ultimate goal regarding the body? Can you do this and be immoral?

• Look at every place you underlined *do you not know* and see what Paul expected his readers to know.

OBSERVE

Leader: *Read aloud Ephesians 5:3, reprinted on the next page.*

   • *Have the group draw a cloud around the words* **immorality** *and* **impurity.**

INSIGHT

A *saint* is a sanctified believer—pure, holy, and blameless in heart and life. The word *saint* comes from the same root word in the Greek as *holy.* It means "to be set apart, consecrated to God."

17 But the one who joins himself to the Lord is one spirit with Him.

18 Flee immorality. Every other sin that a man commits is outside the body, but the immoral man sins against his own body.

19 Or do you not know that your body is a temple of the Holy Spirit who is in you, whom you have from God, and that you are not your own?

20 For you have been bought with a price: therefore glorify God in your body.

EPHESIANS 5:3

But immorality or any impurity or greed must not even be named among you, as is proper among saints.

DISCUSS

• What did you learn from this verse about immorality and the believer?

• Taking into consideration all the scriptures you've looked at this week, discuss the standard God has set for the believer and why immorality seems to be such a problem among Christian men.

• Through this study, have you felt convicted about any behaviors in your life? Take some time to talk privately with God and confess any sin, if necessary.

WRAP IT UP

Through this week's study we've seen that the will of God for the believer is sanctification. We are to live holy, pure, upright, blameless lives. Sexual immorality—adultery, fornication, lustful passions, sexual fantasizing, embracing sexually impure thoughts or images—defiles the body and the marriage bed. Of all sins, the sexual ones can cause the most damage to an intimate relationship with God, with spouses, and with fellow believers.

Holiness. Absolute purity. This is the standard for the believer. How in the world can a man overcome the fiery, powerful passions that challenge his firm commitment to live righteously? Wonderfully, God has not left us on our own to accomplish this.

God gave us the Bible so we could know the standard. If you learn its precepts, call them to mind in times of temptation, and choose to obey them without hesitation, then you will experience sanctification. We have been instructed on how we ought to walk and please God. Each of us is to "know how to possess his own vessel in sanctification and honor" (1 Thessalonians 4:4).

Marriage, as Paul noted, can satisfy a man's sexual passions through an intimate relationship with his wife. In addition to honoring her before men, this allows a man to be holy before God. If he violates this principle, God will judge and avenge any illicit actions.

God also gave every believer, married or single, the Holy Spirit to convict us of sin and lead us in the ways of righteousness.

Yet despite all of this, staggering numbers of believers are falling into sexual immorality. What's the problem? Are men doomed to failure in this area? Are we incapable of successfully living a life of holiness? How can we possibly please God amid a culture that advocates sexual immorality as a man's right?

If you want to know the answers to these questions, then don't miss the next five weeks.

As we saw in last week's lesson, God requires that we live a life that is holy, pure, upright, and blameless. We are to reverence Him in all we do and turn away from evil at every occurrence. And He equipped us with the power of His Holy Spirit, who dwells within us, and His Word, which tells us how to please Him.

So why do we struggle between living in the flesh and walking in the Spirit?

The answer is that we have an enemy who wants us to make wrong choices and who will go to great extremes in enticing us toward failure.

Who is this enemy? What are his weapons? Where does he attack the believer? And what is his battle plan? Let's see what the Bible has to say about these questions.

OBSERVE

Leader: *Read aloud Job 1:1-5.*

• *Circle every reference to **Job**, including pronouns.*

DISCUSS

• What did you learn from marking *Job*? How would you describe him?

JOB 1:1-5

¹ There was a man in the land of Uz whose name was Job; and that man was blameless, upright, fearing God and turning away from evil.

² Seven sons and three daughters were born to him.

³ His possessions also were 7,000 sheep,

3,000 camels, 500 yoke of oxen, 500 female donkeys, and very many servants; and that man was the greatest of all the men of the east.

⁴ His sons used to go and hold a feast in the house of each one on his day, and they would send and invite their three sisters to eat and drink with them.

⁵ When the days of feasting had completed their cycle, Job would send and consecrate them, rising up early in the morning and offering burnt offerings according to the number of them all; for Job said, "Perhaps my sons have sinned and cursed God in their hearts." Thus Job did continually.

• Last week we learned from 1 Thessalonians 4:1-8 that the will of God for the believer is his sanctification. Did Job live a sanctified life before God? How do you know?

OBSERVE

Leader: Read aloud Job 1:6-12. Have the group…

- *draw a pitchfork over every reference to **Satan**, like this:* ⅂
- *circle every reference to **Job**, including pronouns.*

DISCUSS

- Briefly describe what is taking place in this passage and who is involved.

- Would God describe you as He described Job?

- What did you learn from marking the references to Satan? What was Satan's attitude toward Job?

JOB 1:6-12

6 Now there was a day when the sons of God came to present themselves before the LORD, and Satan also came among them.

7 The LORD said to Satan, "From where do you come?" Then Satan answered the LORD and said, "From roaming about on the earth and walking around on it."

8 The LORD said to Satan, "Have you considered My servant Job? For there is no one like him on the earth, a blameless and upright man, fearing God and turning away from evil."

9 Then Satan answered the LORD,

"Does Job fear God for nothing?

10 "Have You not made a hedge about him and his house and all that he has, on every side? You have blessed the work of his hands, and his possessions have increased in the land.

11 "But put forth Your hand now and touch all that he has; he will surely curse You to Your face."

12 Then the LORD said to Satan, "Behold, all that he has is in your power, only do not put forth your hand on him." So Satan departed from the presence of the LORD.

• According to Satan, why did Job reverence God?

• What did Satan propose in respect to Job in verses 10 and 11?

• According to verse 12, is Satan's power limited? If so, in what way?

OBSERVE

Leader: *Read aloud Job 1:13-22.*

- *Circle every reference to **Job,** including pronouns.*
- *Underline each occurrence of the phrase **I alone have escaped to tell you.***

DISCUSS

- What did Job lose and in what time frame?

- What, if anything, had Job done to deserve these catastrophes?

JOB 1:13-22

13 Now on the day when his sons and his daughters were eating and drinking wine in their oldest brother's house,

14 a messenger came to Job and said, "The oxen were plowing and the donkeys feeding beside them,

15 and the Sabeans attacked and took them. They also slew the servants with the edge of the sword, and I alone have escaped to tell you."

16 While he was still speaking, another also came and said, "The fire of God fell from heaven and burned up the sheep and the servants and consumed them, and I alone have escaped to tell you."

17 While he was still speaking, another also came and said, "The Chaldeans formed three bands and made a raid on the camels and took them and slew the servants with the edge of the sword, and I alone have escaped to tell you."

18 While he was still speaking, another also came and said, "Your sons and your daughters were eating and drinking wine in their oldest brother's house,

19 and behold, a great wind came from across the wilderness and struck the four corners of the house, and it fell on the young people and they died, and I alone have escaped to tell you."

• What was Job's reaction to these unexpected tragedies?

• Look back at Job 1:11. What had Satan hoped Job's reaction would be?

• Satan ruined Job's financial and family life, but what was he ultimately trying to destroy?

• How do you respond to tragedy and adversity?

OBSERVE

We are engaged in a war. Our enemy is the devil himself. As the story of Job indicates, his objective is to destroy our relationship with God.

Leader: Read aloud 1 Peter 5:8.
  • *Draw a pitchfork over every reference to* ***the devil.***

INSIGHT

The word *devour* is translated from the Greek verb *katapino,* from the preposition *kata,* meaning "down," and the verb *pino,* meaning "to eat or drink." So this could be rendered as "eat down." The word *devour* gives us a picture of the devil attempting to consume the believer by his destructive tactics so that he is rendered ineffective in his walk before God and in his service to Him.

---

20 Then Job arose and tore his robe and shaved his head, and he fell to the ground and worshiped.

21 He said, "Naked I came from my mother's womb, and naked I shall return there. The LORD gave and the LORD has taken away. Blessed be the name of the LORD."

22 Through all this Job did not sin nor did he blame God.

1 PETER 5:8

Be of sober spirit, be on the alert. Your adversary, the devil, prowls around like a roaring lion, seeking someone to devour.

DISCUSS

• What did you learn about the devil from this verse?

• Have you ever felt "consumed"— overwhelmed or flooded—by sexually impure thoughts?

• During this time how did you view yourself? What were your thoughts regarding your relationship with God?

EPHESIANS 6:10-13

10 Finally, be strong in the Lord and in the strength of His might.

11 Put on the full armor of God, so that you will be able to stand firm against the schemes of the devil.

OBSERVE

Leader: Read aloud Ephesians 6:10-13. Have the group do the following:

• *Draw a box around each occurrence of the phrase **the full armor of God.***
• *Mark each reference to **the devil** with a pitchfork.*
• *Underline each occurrence of the phrase **stand firm.***

OBSERVE

Leader: Read aloud verse 12 again.

- *This time have the group number each of **the enemies the believer struggles against.** (The first—"the rulers"—is numbered for you.)*

DISCUSS

- From what you read in this passage, who is the believer struggling against?

- According to verse 11, what is the believer to stand firm against?

INSIGHT

The *schemes* mentioned in verse 11 are orderly, deceptive procedures used by the devil. Each stage of the deception process is well planned, in the hope of causing maximum damage to the victim's relationship with God.

The word *struggle* in verse 12 indicates hand-to-hand combat.

12 For our struggle is not against flesh and blood, but against the ① rulers, against the powers, against the world forces of this darkness, against the spiritual forces of wickedness in the heavenly places.

13 Therefore, take up the full armor of God, so that you will be able to resist in the evil day, and having done everything, to stand firm.

• What commands is the believer given in this passage?

• If he does what he is commanded, what will the believer be able to do?

• From these verses and the information in the Insight box, who bears the responsibility of making sure you are outfitted for this hand-to-hand combat?

• Where can you find the strength to stand firm?

2 CORINTHIANS 10:3-5

3 For though we walk in the flesh, we do not war according to the flesh,

4 for the weapons of our warfare are not of the flesh, but divinely powerful for the destruction of fortresses.

OBSERVE

Leader: Read aloud 2 Corinthians 10:3-5. Have the group...

- *circle every reference to* **believers,** *which is indicated by the pronoun* **we.**
- *mark each occurrence of the word* **flesh** *with a slash, like this:* ╱
- *underline the words* **war** *and* **warfare.**

DISCUSS

• What did you learn about the believer by marking *we*?

• What did you learn by marking *flesh*?

• What kind of war are we fighting—physical or spiritual? Explain your answer from the text.

• What does it mean to "walk in the flesh" but not to "war according to the flesh"?

INSIGHT

The word *fortresses* in verse 4 refers to entrenched principles that guide one's life. In this particular context it indicates improper mindsets that come from embracing and accepting false teachings and that develop into a mental stronghold of untruths.

Speculations refers to a man using only his intellect and experience to evaluate something rather than considering God's mind on the matter.

---

5 We are destroying speculations and every lofty thing raised up against the knowledge of God, and we are taking every thought captive to the obedience of Christ.

• Where is our battle fought, according to this passage?

• What are we to take captive?

• How can the world's view on sexual promiscuity become a fortress in your life? a speculation?

• What fortresses or speculations have you taken "captive to the obedience of Christ"?

OBSERVE

We began this week's study with Job, who was described as being blameless, upright, fearing God, and turning away from evil. Yet, like most men, he had to deal with sexually impure thoughts. Let's return to Job to see what he did to guard against sexual temptations.

Leader: *Read aloud Job 31:1,7,9-12. Have the group do the following:*

- *Circle each reference to* **Job.** *Since he is speaking in this passage, the pronouns* **I** *and* **my** *refer to him.*
- *Draw a cloud around any word or phrase that refers to* **a sexually impure thought, desire,** *or* **action.**
- *Draw a heart like this* ♡ *over every occurrence of the word* **heart.**

INSIGHT

In verse 1, *gaze* is translated from a Hebrew word that means "to carefully observe or pay close attention to." It indicates examining with the eyes, thinking about what is seen, and processing the information for the purposes of implementing a response. A gaze is far more than just a casual, unintended, unavoidable glance.

JOB 31:1,7,9-12

1 "I have made a covenant with my eyes; how then could I gaze at a virgin?

7 "If my step has turned from the way, or my heart followed my eyes, or if any spot has stuck to my hands,

9 "if my heart has been enticed by a woman, or I have lurked at my neighbor's doorway,

10 may my wife grind for another, and let others kneel down over her.

11 "For that would be a lustful crime; moreover, it would be an iniquity punishable by judges.

12 "For it would be fire that consumes to Abaddon, and would uproot all my increase."

DISCUSS

• What did you learn by marking the references to Job?

• What did you learn from drawing a cloud around the references to sexually impure thoughts, desires, or actions? How can you apply each truth to your own life?

• According to verse 1, what did Job do to prevent himself from lusting after any women he encountered?

• Did he make this choice before or after the virgin came on the scene?

• In verse 7, what connection did Job make between the eyes and the heart? Why would that be significant?

• What is your first line of defense against falling into the temptation of sexual immorality?

• According to Job, what consequences might come from having sex with someone other than your wife?

WRAP IT UP

Job was doing everything right: He was blameless and upright. He feared God and turned away from evil. He held fast to his integrity, even in temptation. His life was pleasing to God. His relationship with God seemed invincible—and then Satan came to call.

How would you measure up in similar circumstances? Is your commitment to purity firm?

We battle against a spiritual enemy—the devil. Our war is not against flesh and blood but against spiritual forces. Satan fights us at every opportunity. He roams the earth, seeking someone to devour. His passion is for us to curse God to His face rather than praise Him for who He is. Satan will command his rulers, use his powers, and send forth his spiritual forces of wickedness upon us without a moment's notice. He will do everything he can to change our mind about the God we worship and make us forget or ignore the instructions God has given to us. Our spiritual defeat is his victory.

He wants to weaken you through a devastating onslaught of temptation and persuade you to rethink your views on how to live before God.

He wants to make you so miserable that you abandon your trust in God.

He wants to inflict upon you disheartening circumstances so that you'll sit down in the ashes of a burned-out life and refuse to obey God.

He wants to torture you with innumerable painful experiences and cause you to blame God and turn your back on Him.

Satan's hatred knows no bounds—except that he's restricted by

God's boundless power working through us. We can stand firm in the Lord and in the strength of His might. We can wage war with the divinely powerful spiritual weapons that God has provided for us, the full armor of God. We can make and keep a covenant with our eyes. We can take captive any thought that is raised up against the knowledge of God, any consideration that is not true according to God's Word.

That is how we resist the devil and prevent him from establishing his deceptive fortresses of falsehood in our minds. That is how we stand firm against him and his schemes.

When we do this, like Job we will be victorious in the battle that is waged in and for the mind of man.

In last week's study, we learned that we are in a battle against the spiritual forces of wickedness.

This week we want to get a better understanding of our enemy and his tactics. What is he like? What are some of his characteristics? How does he operate? How does he fight? How can we recognize his traps?

We'll start by examining some verses that describe his methods, then look at how this played out in his encounters with Jesus and David.

OBSERVE

Leader: Read aloud Revelation 12:9.

- *Have the group mark all references to **the great dragon,** including any synonyms or pronouns, with a pitchfork:*

REVELATION 12:9

And the great dragon was thrown down, the serpent of old who is called the devil and Satan, who deceives the whole world; he was thrown down to the earth, and his angels were thrown down with him.

INSIGHT

The word *deceives* in this verse means "to seduce away from the truth, to cause to err, or to lead one to form a wrong judgment."

DISCUSS

- What did you learn about the devil? What does he do?

• In what ways is Satan deceiving men and women in the area of sexuality?

2 CORINTHIANS 11: 3

But I am afraid that, as the serpent deceived Eve by his craftiness, your minds will be led astray from the simplicity and purity of devotion to Christ.

OBSERVE

Leader: *Read aloud 2 Corinthians 11:3.*
> • *Have the group mark* **serpent** *and any pronouns with a pitchfork, as before.*

DISCUSS

• What did you learn about the serpent?

• What in a believer's life is the target of the serpent's deception?

INSIGHT

The word *craftiness* describes how the devil deceives. He employs any method he can to achieve his goal. His tactics are cunning, shrewd, and unscrupulous.

• What was Paul concerned that the Corinthian believers would be led astray from?

• What are some of the methods the devil uses to seduce the minds of men in the sexual realm?

OBSERVE

In this next verse, Jesus is speaking to religious leaders who refuse to believe He is the Son of God.

Leader: Read aloud John 8:44.
  • *Have the group mark every reference to* **the devil**, *including any synonyms or pronouns, with a pitchfork.*

DISCUSS

• What did you learn from marking the references to the devil?

• What has been his character from the beginning? How does he accomplish his purposes?

JOHN 8:44

You are of your father the devil, and you want to do the desires of your father. He was a murderer from the beginning, and does not stand in the truth because there is no truth in him. Whenever he speaks a lie, he speaks from his own nature, for he is a liar and the father of lies.

• What are some of the enemy's lies men believe today concerning sexuality?

• Men are often tempted not only with impure heterosexual thoughts but also with homosexual thoughts, causing some to think, *I must be perverted!* or *I must be gay!* Discuss what this reflects about the enemy and his tactics.

MATTHEW 4:1-11

¹ Then Jesus was led up by the Spirit into the wilderness to be tempted by the devil.

² And after He had fasted forty days and forty nights, He then became hungry.

³ And the tempter came and said to Him,

OBSERVE

Let's observe how Jesus responded to one of Satan's attacks of deception.

Leader: Read aloud Matthew 4:1-11. Have the group do the following:
- *Underline every reference to **Jesus**, including any synonyms and pronouns.*
- *Mark references to **the devil**, including pronouns, with a pitchfork, as before.*
- *Draw a box around each occurrence of the phrase **it is written**.*

DISCUSS

- Briefly discuss what is happening in these verses, where it is happening, and who is involved.

- As you look at the devil's first temptation of Jesus found in verses 2-4, what aspect of the flesh did the devil appeal to? (Note the connection between the temptation and Jesus' condition in verse 2.)

- Have you ever rationalized satisfying your sexual appetite in a way that goes against the Word of God?

- Discuss the second temptation found in verses 5-7. What was the devil tempting Jesus to do? What reason did he offer?

- In verse 7, how did Jesus respond when the devil quoted one of God's promises?

"If You are the Son of God, command that these stones become bread."

4 But He answered and said, "It is written, 'Man shall not live on bread alone, but on every word that proceeds out of the mouth of God.'"

5 Then the devil took Him into the holy city and had Him stand on the pinnacle of the temple,

6 and said to Him, "If You are the Son of God, throw Yourself down; for it is written, 'He will command His angels concerning You'; and 'On their hands they will bear You up, So that You will not strike Your foot against a stone.'"

7 Jesus said to him, "On the other hand, it is written, 'You shall not put the LORD your God to the test.'"

8 Again, the devil took Him to a very high mountain and showed Him all the kingdoms of the world and their glory;

9 and he said to Him, "All these things I will give You, if You fall down and worship me."

10 Then Jesus said to him, "Go, Satan! For it is written, 'You shall worship the LORD your God, and serve Him only.'"

11 Then the devil left Him; and behold, angels came and began to minister to Him.

• Have you ever presumptuously committed a sin, planning in advance to take advantage of God's promise of forgiveness, while choosing to ignore numerous verses commanding you to walk by the Spirit and abstain from fleshly lusts?

• Would that be putting "the Lord your God to the test"? Explain your answer.

• Discuss the third temptation in verses 8-10. What was the devil offering Jesus?

• Jesus had come to earth to die for the sins of man, then rise from the dead and ascend into heaven, returning one day to rule the world. If Jesus had accepted the devil's offer, what would He have bypassed? What would be the cost of His doing so?

• Have you ever been tempted to break God's laws regarding sex and marriage because you wanted the immediate gratification the world had to offer? If you gave in to that temptation, whom would you be worshiping?

• Look back at every place you marked *it is written.* Discuss how Jesus handled each temptation and how you can follow His example.

• When the devil tempts you with a thought that is contrary to the Word of God, how should you respond?

OBSERVE

An intimate knowledge of the Word of God is a crucial weapon in our battle against the enemy. It's also helpful to understand Satan's plan of attack, which is revealed in the following passage.

Leader: Read James 1:13-15. Have the group…
  • *underline every reference to **mankind,** including the phrases **no one** and **each one** and the pronouns **I, his,** and **he** (when not capitalized to indicate God).*
  • *mark each occurrence of the words **tempted** and **tempt** with a check mark: ✓*

JAMES 1:13-15

13 Let no one say when he is tempted, "I am being tempted by God"; for God cannot be tempted by evil, and He Himself does not tempt anyone.

14 But each one is tempted when he is carried away and enticed by his own lust.

15 Then when lust has conceived, it gives birth to sin; and when sin is accomplished, it brings forth death.

DISCUSS

• What did you learn from underlining the references to mankind?

• What did you learn from marking the references to temptation?

OBSERVE

Leader: *Read James 1:13-15 again. This time have the group...*

> • *mark each occurrence of the word **sin** with a big* **S,** *like a serpent.*
> • *draw a cloud around each occurrence of the word **lust.***

INSIGHT

The word *enticed,* found in verse 14, is a term used in fishing and hunting. It gives a word picture of luring a fish from its hiding place or an animal into a trap.

DISCUSS

• According to this passage, is it a sin to be tempted? Explain your answer.

• What events lead to sin?

• What is the end result of sin?

• What are some "deaths" that could come into a man's life from yielding to his lust?

OBSERVE

The devil presents his lies and deceptions in very attractive ways, enticing unsuspecting prey to ponder the temptation and consider it right and justifiable. He hopes that the desire to take the luscious bait will be irresistible. He whispers, "Go ahead. It's all right."

Let's see how the enemy used this tactic in the life of King David.

2 SAMUEL 11:1-5

¹ Then it happened in the spring, at the time when kings go out to battle, that David sent Joab and his servants with him and all Israel, and they destroyed the sons of Ammon and besieged Rabbah. But David stayed at Jerusalem.

² Now when evening came David arose from his bed and walked around on the roof of the king's house, and from the roof he saw a woman bathing; and the woman was very beautiful in appearance.

³ So David sent and inquired about the woman. And one said, "Is this not Bathsheba,

Leader: Read aloud 2 Samuel 11:1-5. Have the group…

- *underline every reference to **David**, including the pronouns.*
- *circle every reference to **Bathsheba**, including **woman** and any pronouns.*

INSIGHT

The Hebrew word translated as *saw* in verse 2 does not indicate a casual glance. It means "to look at something intently, to inspect, to examine."

DISCUSS

- Describe the progression of events in this incident in David's life.

- What options were available to David when he first saw Bathsheba? What actions could he have taken that would have led away from temptation?

• What options are available to you when you see a beautiful woman other than your wife in skimpy clothing or a tight-fitting outfit?

• What course of action would lead you away from temptation?

• According to verse 3, did David have a second chance to resist the temptation?

• Think back to what we learned in James 1:13-15. How is the progression that leads to sin illustrated in David's story?

the daughter of Eliam, the wife of Uriah the Hittite?"

⁴ David sent messengers and took her, and when she came to him, he lay with her; and when she had purified herself from her uncleanness, she returned to her house.

⁵ The woman conceived; and she sent and told David, and said, "I am pregnant."

OBSERVE

The passage we'll examine next describes the scene when Nathan the prophet confronts David, exposing his sin with Bathsheba—a sin the king thought he had covered up.

2 SAMUEL 12:7-14

7 Nathan then said to David, "You are the man! Thus says the LORD God of Israel, 'It is I who anointed you king over Israel and it is I who delivered you from the hand of Saul.

8 'I also gave you your master's house and your master's wives into your care, and I gave you the house of Israel and Judah; and if that had been too little, I would have added to you many more things like these!

9 'Why have you despised the word of the LORD by doing evil in His sight? You have struck down Uriah the Hittite with the sword, have taken

Leader: Read aloud 2 Samuel 12:7-14. Have the group…

- *mark every reference to **God**, including the pronoun **I**, with a triangle:* △
- *underline every reference to **David**, including pronouns.*

DISCUSS

- What did you learn from marking *God* and *David*?

OBSERVE

Leader: Read aloud these verses again. This time have the group…

- *mark every reference to **sin** and **evil** with a big **S** as before.*
- *draw a tombstone over the word **die**, like this:* ⌂

DISCUSS

• Keeping in mind what you learned from James 1:13-15, what came as a result of David's yielding to temptation?

• According to verse 9, what had David despised when he did evil in God's sight?

his wife to be your wife, and have killed him with the sword of the sons of Ammon.

10 'Now therefore, the sword shall never depart from your house, because you have despised Me and have taken the wife of Uriah the Hittite to be your wife.'

11 "Thus says the LORD, 'Behold, I will raise up evil against you from your own household; I will even take your wives before your eyes and give them to your companion, and he will lie with your wives in broad daylight.

12 'Indeed you did it secretly, but I will do this thing before all Israel, and under the sun.'"

13 Then David said to Nathan, "I have sinned against the LORD." And Nathan said to David, "The LORD also has taken away your sin; you shall not die.

14 "However, because by this deed you have given occasion to the enemies of the LORD to blaspheme, the child also that is born to you shall surely die."

• Explain how this is true for any believer who chooses to give in to temptation.

OBSERVE

Leader: *Have the group read aloud with you Numbers 32:23.*

NUMBERS 32:23

"Behold, you have sinned against the LORD, and be sure your sin will find you out."

DISCUSS

• Based on everything you've learned up to this point, do you think a believer can get away with sexual immorality? Discuss your reasoning.

• Discuss some practical ways to prevent temptation from leading to lust and then to sin and death.

WRAP IT UP

The devil is the chief deceiver, the father of all lies. And he is the tempter. He entices the believer to abandon his relationship with God through disbelief and disobedience.

Satan's strategy is to put attractive things before our eyes, appealing thoughts in our minds, and passions in our souls to prompt us to follow what seems right to our eyes, justifiable to our reasoning, and pleasurable to our flesh.

If we give in to these temptations, we will pay the price. Yielding to the devil's deceptions will take us further than we ever thought we'd go, keep us longer than we ever thought we'd stay, and cost us more than we ever thought we'd have to pay.

The pain of sin affects all involved, not just the offender, as David's story so clearly reveals. Ask anyone who has despised the grace and goodness of God in order to chase after momentary pleasure. They can enumerate for you the "deaths" that took place as a result of their choices.

Temptations do not inevitably result in sin. Through the power of the Holy Spirit and God's Word, we can halt the progression from temptation to the conception of sin. As Jesus' encounter with Satan demonstrates, rather than despising the Word of God, we can use it to reveal the enemy's lies. We can choose not to be carried away and enticed by our own lust. We can control our appetites. And we can have everything the next world offers by resisting the temptation to settle for the temporary things of this present world.

Our success will be determined by our response when Satan attacks. Are you fully prepared for battle?

Why is sexual immorality so attractive and appealing at times? Why are men drawn to respond inappropriately to a flirtatious woman?

How can you keep your dreams pure and your thoughts above reproach when you are inundated with sexually explicit images day and night? You see them via the media as well as through live encounters with improperly dressed women in the workplace and elsewhere?

What will an adulterous affair cost you? Are you prepared to pay the price?

What can you do to protect yourself from the temptations of a sexually aggressive woman?

As we seek to address these questions, let's see what wisdom we can gain from a father's advice to his son.

OBSERVE

Leader: Read aloud Proverbs 5:1-14. Have the group...

- *underline every reference to **the son(s),** including pronouns.*
- *draw a cloud around each reference to **the adulteress,** including pronouns that refer to this immoral woman.*

DISCUSS

- What did you learn about the adulteress and her ways?

PROVERBS 5:1-14

1 My son, give attention to my wisdom, incline your ear to my understanding;

2 that you may observe discretion and your lips may reserve knowledge.

3 For the lips of an adulteress drip honey and smoother than oil is her speech;

4 but in the end she is bitter as wormwood, sharp as a two-edged sword.

5 Her feet go down to death, her steps take hold of Sheol.

6 She does not ponder the path of life; her ways are unstable, she does not know it.

7 Now then, my sons, listen to me and do not depart from the words of my mouth.

8 Keep your way far from her and do not go near the door of her house,

9 or you will give your vigor to others and your years to the cruel one;

10 and strangers will be filled with your

• Look at every reference to the son and discuss what you learned.

• What specific instructions in this passage would help you avoid immorality?

• What are the consequences of not heeding these instructions?

strength and your hard-earned goods will go to the house of an alien;

11 and you groan at your final end, when your flesh and your body are consumed;

12 and you say, "How I have hated instruction! And my heart spurned reproof!

13 "I have not listened to the voice of my teachers, nor inclined my ear to my instructors!

14 "I was almost in utter ruin in the midst of the assembly and congregation."

PROVERBS 6:20-35

20 My son, observe the commandment of your father and do not forsake the teaching of your mother;

21 bind them continually on your heart; tie them around your neck.

22 When you walk about, they will guide you; when you sleep, they will watch over you; and when you awake, they will talk to you.

23 For the commandment is a lamp and the teaching is light; and reproofs for discipline are the way of life

24 to keep you from the evil woman, from the smooth tongue of the adulteress.

OBSERVE

Leader: Read aloud Proverbs 6:20-35. Have the group…

- *underline* **my son** *and any pronouns that refer to him, as well as the phrases* **a man** *and* **the one.**
- *draw a cloud around every reference to* **the evil woman** *or* **the adulteress,** *including any synonyms and pronouns that refer to her.*

INSIGHT

The word *wounds* in verse 33 is translated from the Hebrew word *nega,* which means "stroke, plaque, or disease." *Nega* comes from the root word *naga,* which means "to touch" or "that which pertains when one thing (or person) physically contacts another."[1]

---

1 R. L. Harris, G. L. Archer, Jr., and B. K. Waltke, *Theological Wordbook of the Old Testament* (electronic ed.), (Chicago: Moody Press; 1980, 1999), 552.

DISCUSS

• In this passage, what are the father's instructions to his son?

• To what does he compare adultery in verses 27-29?

25 Do not desire her beauty in your heart, nor let her capture you with her eyelids.

26 For on account of a harlot one is reduced to a loaf of bread, and an adulteress hunts for the precious life.

27 Can a man take fire in his bosom and his clothes not be burned?

28 Or can a man walk on hot coals and his feet not be scorched?

29 So is the one who goes in to his neighbor's wife; whoever touches her will not go unpunished.

30 Men do not despise a thief if he steals to satisfy himself when he is hungry;

31 but when he is found, he must repay sevenfold; he must give all the substance of his house.

32 The one who commits adultery with a woman is lacking sense; he who would destroy himself does it.

33 Wounds and disgrace he will find, and his reproach will not be blotted out.

34 For jealousy enrages a man, and he will not spare in the day of vengeance.

35 He will not accept any ransom, nor will he be satisfied though you give many gifts.

• What did you learn about this evil woman, the adulteress? How does she attract a man?

• According to this passage, what are the consequences of adultery?

OBSERVE

Leader: *Read aloud Proverbs 7:1-27. Have the group do the following:*

- *Underline every reference to **the son(s)**, including pronouns.*
- *Draw a cloud around every reference to **the adulteress**, including any pronouns or synonyms.*
- *Starting at verse 7, draw a box around every reference to **the young man**.*

DISCUSS

- What did you learn from marking the references to the adulteress?

PROVERBS 7:1-27

1 My son, keep my words and treasure my commandments within you.

2 Keep my commandments and live, and my teaching as the apple of your eye.

3 Bind them on your fingers; write them on the tablet of your heart.

4 Say to wisdom, "You are my sister," and call understanding your intimate friend;

5 that they may keep you from an adulteress, from the foreigner who flatters with her words.

6 For at the window of my house I looked out through my lattice,

7 and I saw among the naive, and discerned among the youths a young man lacking sense,

8 passing through the street near her corner; and he takes the way to her house,

9 in the twilight, in the evening, in the middle of the night and in the darkness.

10 And behold, a woman comes to meet him, dressed as a harlot and cunning of heart.

11 She is boisterous and rebellious, her feet do not remain at home;

12 she is now in the streets, now in the squares, and lurks by every corner.

• What makes this woman enticing?

• From verses 7-23, what did you learn about this young man? How is he described? What gets him in trouble?

- Describe the woman he encountered. How does she lure him into sin?

- In our society, where does a man encounter these kinds of women?

13 So she seizes him and kisses him and with a brazen face she says to him:

14 "I was due to offer peace offerings; today I have paid my vows.

15 "Therefore I have come out to meet you, to seek your presence earnestly, and I have found you.

16 "I have spread my couch with coverings, with colored linens of Egypt.

17 "I have sprinkled my bed with myrrh, aloes and cinnamon.

18 "Come, let us drink our fill of love until morning; let us delight ourselves with caresses.

19 "For my husband is not at home, he has gone on a long journey;

20 he has taken a bag of money with him, at the full moon he will come home."

21 With her many persuasions she entices him; with her flattering lips she seduces him.

22 Suddenly he follows her as an ox goes to the slaughter, or as one in fetters to the discipline of a fool,

23 until an arrow pierces through his liver; as a bird hastens to the snare, so he does not know that it will cost him his life.

• According to this passage, what is a man's protection against a woman on the hunt?

• According to verses 25-27, where will immorality lead a man?

24 Now therefore, my sons, listen to me, and pay attention to the words of my mouth.

25 Do not let your heart turn aside to her ways, do not stray into her paths.

26 For many are the victims she has cast down, and numerous are all her slain.

27 Her house is the way to Sheol, descending to the chambers of death.

OBSERVE

Leader: Read aloud Proverbs 5:15-23. Have the group do the following:
- *Underline the pronouns **your, you,** and **my son.** Also underline **a man** and the pronouns relating to him in verses 21-23.*
- *Once again, draw a cloud around the words **adulteress** and **foreigner.***

PROVERBS 5:15-23

15 Drink water from your own cistern and fresh water from your own well.

16 Should your springs be dispersed abroad, streams of water in the streets?

17 Let them be yours alone and not for strangers with you.

18 Let your fountain be blessed, and rejoice in the wife of your youth.

19 As a loving hind and a graceful doe, let her breasts satisfy you at all times; be exhilarated always with her love.

20 For why should you, my son, be exhilarated with an adulteress and embrace the bosom of a foreigner?

21 For the ways of a man are before the eyes of the LORD, and He watches all his paths.

22 His own iniquities will capture the wicked, and he will be held with the cords of his sin.

INSIGHT

In the context of Proverbs 5, the word *cistern* is used figuratively in verse 15, referring to a man's wife as his well of living water. This is where a man finds total satisfaction, quenching all of his sexual thirst.

DISCUSS

• Where is a man instructed to satisfy his sexual thirst? Where is he *not* to go?

• What do you learn from verses 21-23 about a man's actions? What is the outcome when he ignores instruction?

- Discuss how pornography functions like the cords of sin mentioned in verse 22.

23 He will die for lack of instruction, and in the greatness of his folly he will go astray.

- Drawing on all you've learned from Proverbs 5–7, summarize what we can do to avoid an encounter with the adulteress, how we can recognize her, and what the consequences will be if we choose to ignore the wisdom of these passages.

WRAP IT UP

In 1 Thessalonians 4:1-2, a passage we studied in week 1, we read Paul's instructions to the Thessalonian believers regarding how they ought to walk and please God—how to live a sanctified life. We have seen that same principle emphasized this week in our study in Proverbs: Know the Word of God and keep His commandments. According to Proverbs 7:5, knowing and following God's Word will help you avoid the snare of an adulteress.

The adulteress is on the prowl, seeking to entrap the foolish man. Her words are like honey, and she knows how to say what a man wants to hear. She lurks in the streets of life, waiting for the naive to come by and be enticed by her persuasions.

If we succumb to the flattery of this unfaithful woman, the consequences are severe:

- Our strength will go to strangers.
- Our hard-earned goods will go to the house of an alien.
- Our folly will expose us to sexually transmitted diseases.
- Our lack of discipline will bring an addiction that binds.
- Our sin will not go unpunished.

My son, listen to the Father and do not depart from the words of His mouth. Our ways are ever before His eyes, and He is watching all that we do. Observe His commandments and live. Stay far away from the adulteress and do not go near the door of her house.

You have been instructed, and you know what to do. You stand without excuse from this day forward. Will you choose the path of wisdom or the path of destruction?

As we've seen in our study these past few weeks, we are fighting a fierce spiritual battle against an enemy who is powerful and deceptive. He is waging an all-out war to destroy our relationship with God, and the lure of sexual temptation is one of his most effective means of attack.

By what means can we resist the tactics and temptations of the devil? How can we achieve victory over the temptations of sexual immorality?

We'll explore the answers to those questions in this week's study, as we observe the example of Joseph, a man who faced great pressures in the area of sexual temptation.

OBSERVE

The enemy often presses his advantage when we are away from home, convincing us that no one will ever know if we give in to temptation "just this once." Joseph found himself in just such a situation after his brothers, out of jealousy, sold him into slavery. Far from home, it would have been easy for him to toss aside his faith and its standards for life, believing that no one would care about his choices. We pick up the story in Genesis 39.

Leader: *Read aloud Genesis 39:1-6. Have the group do the following:*

GENESIS 39:1-6

1 Now Joseph had been taken down to Egypt; and Potiphar, an Egyptian officer of Pharaoh, the captain of the bodyguard, bought him from the Ishmaelites, who had taken him down there.

2 The LORD was with Joseph, so he became a successful man. And he was in the house of his master, the Egyptian.

3 Now his master saw that the LORD was with him and how the LORD caused all that he did to prosper in his hand.

4 So Joseph found favor in his sight and became his personal servant; and he made him overseer over his house, and all that he owned he put in his charge.

5 It came about that from the time he made him overseer in his house and over all that he owned, the LORD blessed the Egyptian's house on account of Joseph; thus the LORD's blessing was upon all that he owned, in the house and in the field.

• *Circle every reference to **Joseph**, including pronouns.*
• *Put a **P** over every reference to **Potiphar**.*
• *Draw a box around each occurrence of the phrase **the Lord was with Joseph** or **with him**.*

DISCUSS
• What did you learn about Potiphar and Joseph?

• How would you describe Joseph's relationship with God?

• What description was given of Joseph's physical appearance?

OBSERVE

Leader: Read aloud Genesis 39:7-10. Have the group…

    • *circle every reference to **Joseph**.*

    • *put a **W** over every reference to **Potiphar's wife**, including pronouns.*

    • *draw a cloud* ⛅ *around the phrase* **lie with me.**

DISCUSS

• What did Potiphar's wife propose to Joseph?

6 So he left everything he owned in Joseph's charge; and with him there he did not concern himself with anything except the food which he ate. Now Joseph was handsome in form and appearance.

GENESIS 39:7-10

7 It came about after these events that his master's wife looked with desire at Joseph, and she said, "Lie with me."

8 But he refused and said to his master's wife, "Behold, with me here, my master does not concern himself with anything in the house, and he has put all that he owns in my charge.

9 "There is no one greater in this house

than I, and he has withheld nothing from me except you, because you are his wife. How then could I do this great evil, and sin against God?"

10 As she spoke to Joseph day after day, he did not listen to her to lie beside her or be with her.

• According to the text, what did she do just prior to her proposal?

• How did Joseph respond to her invitation? What reasons did he give her? Be sure to note them all.

• Did she accept his answer and drop the subject? What does this reveal about the persistence of the enemy?

• Have you ever encountered the same temptation day after day? What effect did this have on you?

• Does the text indicate that Joseph had done anything to create this situation with Potiphar's wife?

• Have you ever been tempted by sexual impurity when you were at a spiritual high point in your life?

• Share with the group an example of how your workplace has presented similar temptations.

• What lessons about temptation did you learn from this passage?

• From verse 10, what principle can be drawn from Joseph's life to help us resist sexual temptations?

OBSERVE

Leader: Read aloud Genesis 39:11-16. Once again, have the group...

- *circle every reference to **Joseph**.*
- *put a **W** on every reference to **Potiphar's wife**.*
- *draw a cloud around the phrase **lie with me**.*

DISCUSS

• What was Joseph doing this particular day?

• What seems to be different about the setting inside the house on this day?

GENESIS 39:11-16

11 Now it happened one day that he went into the house to do his work, and none of the men of the household was there inside.

12 She caught him by his garment, saying, "Lie with me!" And he left his garment in her hand and fled, and went outside.

13 When she saw that he had left his garment in her hand and had fled outside,

14 she called to the men of her household and said to them, "See, he has brought in a Hebrew to us to make sport of us; he came in to me to lie with me, and I screamed.

15 "When he heard that I raised my voice and screamed, he left his garment beside me and fled and went outside."

16 So she left his garment beside her until his master came home.

• What, if anything, could Joseph have done to avoid the trap that had been set for him? Explain your answer.

• What did Potiphar's wife do? Do you think Joseph was expecting this to happen?

• What does this reveal about temptations?

• How did Joseph respond to Mrs. Potiphar?

• How did his response differ from their earlier encounters? Would repeating his first response have worked here? Why or why not?

• Do you think Joseph had determined ahead of time how to respond to a situation like this? Explain your answer.

• What lessons can we draw from Joseph's example that would help us successfully avoid an improper sexual encounter?

• What decisions do you need to make today before you are faced with a sudden temptation?

OBSERVE

Leader: Read aloud Genesis 39:17-23. Have the group...

- *continue marking all references to* **Joseph, Potiphar,** *and* **Potiphar's wife,** *as before.*
- *draw a box around each occurrence of the phrase* **the Lord was with Joseph** *or* **with him.**

DISCUSS

- What did Potiphar do when he heard his wife's story?

- Had Joseph done anything wrong?

- Successfully avoiding sexual temptation does not always come with good consequences. Discuss some of the negative consequences Joseph experienced for his choices.

- What consequences might you and other group members face if you found yourselves in a similar situation?

GENESIS 39:17-23

17 Then she spoke to him with these words, "The Hebrew slave, whom you brought to us, came in to me to make sport of me;

18 and as I raised my voice and screamed, he left his garment beside me and fled outside."

19 Now when his master heard the words of his wife, which she spoke to him, saying, "This is what your slave did to me," his anger burned.

20 So Joseph's master took him and put him into the jail, the place where the king's prisoners were confined; and he was there in the jail.

21 But the LORD was with Joseph and extended kindness to him, and gave him favor in the sight of the chief jailer.

22 The chief jailer committed to Joseph's charge all the prisoners who were in the jail; so that whatever was done there, he was responsible for it.

23 The chief jailer did not supervise anything under Joseph's charge because the LORD was with him; and whatever he did, the LORD made to prosper.

• Have you known anyone who was falsely accused of sexual misconduct? What happened?

• Describe Joseph's relationship with the Lord after he was sentenced to an unjust punishment.

• What encouragement does this provide as you determine in advance how to respond to sexual temptation?

OBSERVE

Leader: *Read aloud 1 Corinthians 10:13. Have the group say aloud and...*

- *mark each occurrence of the words* **tempted** *and* **temptation** *with a check mark:* ✓
- *mark the words* **God** *and* **who** *with a triangle:* △

INSIGHT

The word *overtaken* in this context gives a word picture of an emotion or urge that suddenly attempts to seize a person's mind, will, and emotions so that he may be led astray.

1 CORINTHIANS 10:13

No temptation has overtaken you but such as is common to man; and God is faithful, who will not allow you to be tempted beyond what you are able, but with the temptation will provide the way of escape also, so that you will be able to endure it.

DISCUSS

- What did you learn about temptations and being tempted?

- How is God described in this verse? What did you learn about His role in temptation?

• What truths did you learn from this verse that will encourage you the next time you face temptation?

JOB 31:1,7-8

1 "I have made a covenant with my eyes; how then could I gaze at a virgin?

7 "If my step has turned from the way, or my heart followed my eyes, or if any spot has stuck to my hands,

8 "Let me sow and another eat, and let my crops be uprooted."

OBSERVE

As you'll recall from last week's study, David's path toward sin began when he *looked* at Bathsheba and saw that she was beautiful. We also observed that Potiphar's wife *looked* with desire at Joseph just before she attempted to seduce him. Job addressed this connection between the eyes and sexual temptation in the following passage.

Leader: *Read aloud Job 31:1,7-8. Have the group...*
• *circle each **I** and **my,** since these pronouns refer to Job.*
• *draw a heart like this* ♡ *over the word* ***heart.***

INSIGHT

You may recall the definition of the word *gaze* from week 2. It is translated from a Hebrew word that means "to carefully observe or pay close attention to." It indicates examining with the eyes, thinking about what is seen, and processing the information for the purposes of implementing a response. A gaze is far more than just a casual, unintended, unavoidable glance.

DISCUSS

• What did Job do to avoid lusting after other women?

• In addition to temptation, what else does he connect with the eyes?

MATTHEW 5:27-28

27 You have heard that it was said, 'You shall not commit adultery';

28 but I say to you that everyone who looks at a woman with lust for her has already committed adultery with her in his heart.

OBSERVE

Job was aware that the eyes are the doorway to the heart and mind, and Jesus confirmed this same truth.

Leader: Read aloud Matthew 5:27-28. Have the group…
- *draw a cloud around every reference to* **adultery.**
- *underline the words* **looks** *and* **lust.**
- *draw a heart over the word* **heart.**

DISCUSS

- According to these verses, what action constitutes adultery? How does it happen and where does it take place?

INSIGHT

Coupled with the phrase *with lust,* the word *looks* in verse 28 implies a continuous, extended imagining of sexual fantasies with a woman. Once again, it indicates far more than a thoughtless, brief glance.

• In light of the explanation in the Insight box, discuss the principle Jesus is teaching.

• Where does the sin of adultery begin?

• Is lust limited to a person or object within range of sight, or does lust include *looking* at something on the viewing screen of your mind, focusing on it with your thoughts? Explain your answer.

OBSERVE

Leader: Read aloud Proverbs 23:7 and Proverbs 4:23. Have the group…
  • *circle each occurrence of the word **he**.*
  • *mark **within, heart,** and **it** with a heart.*

DISCUSS

• What is the relationship between what a man thinks and who he is and what he does?

PROVERBS 23:7

For as he thinks within himself, so he is.

PROVERBS 4:23

Watch over your heart with all diligence, for from it flow the springs of life.

MARK 7:21-23

21 "For from within, out of the heart of men, proceed the evil thoughts, fornications, thefts, murders, adulteries,

22 "deeds of coveting and wickedness, as well as deceit, sensuality, envy, slander, pride and foolishness.

23 "All these evil things proceed from within and defile the man."

OBSERVE

Leader: *Read aloud Mark 7:21-23.*
  • *Have the group draw a cloud around every **sexual sin** listed.*

DISCUSS

• According to this passage, where do adultery and fornication begin?

• What does this reveal about the necessity of guarding your heart and keeping your thoughts under control?

• How does the principle of guarding your heart apply to the television programs you watch? the movies you see? the magazines you read? the Internet sites you visit? pornography in any form? What guidelines should you follow when women other than your wife cross your line of sight?

Leader: *Lead your group members in a prayer of commitment to God, making a covenant with their eyes not to gaze at other women or think sexually impure thoughts about them.*

WRAP IT UP

God wanted others to know that Joseph was favored by Him, so He prospered everything under the young man's management. Joseph knew how to care for the things God had entrusted to him, and he recognized the danger of touching those things God had entrusted to others. He resisted the passionate pleas of an unfaithful woman, even her subtle requests to "just get together and talk," because he knew that sexual sin is a great evil against God.

Recognizing the danger, Joseph had predetermined to resist Potiphar's wife at every encounter. The only time he was caught off guard is when he entered the house to do his work and none of the men of the household was there. She had set him up for a fall! Such isolated moments are not coincidences; they are a trick of the enemy to ensnare us.

Joseph fled his aggressor but not without cost. His faithfulness to God *and* to Potiphar resulted in imprisonment for a crime he didn't commit. Yet, while doing the right thing resulted in unjust punishment, he did not go to prison alone. The Bible states, "The Lord was with him."

Job is another example of a man committed to following God's standard. He would not look at a woman because he had made a covenant with his eyes. He knew that the eyes are the doorways to the mind, and he knew his heart would follow his eyes. If he saw something he wanted, if it looked good, and if he thought about it long enough, he would figure a way to take hold of it. And he knew this would be wrong in the sight of God.

As the examples of Job and Joseph demonstrate, it is possible to control your thoughts, desires, and passions. You can resist temptation through the power of God, who does not leave us to fight our enemies alone. With each temptation He provides a way of escape so we can endure and come away victorious. He wants others to know we are His, and that message is conveyed not only by what He does for us but also by how we deal with the temptations put before us!

In our study these past few weeks, we've learned that resisting sexual temptation involves guarding our eyes and taking our thoughts captive to the obedience of Christ. The examples of Job and Joseph reveal that it is possible to live the sanctified life, to abstain from both physical and mental acts of sexual immorality.

In this last week of study, we'll explore God's provision for our victory over sexual temptations and discuss some specific actions that will help us keep our thoughts, desires, and passions pure and blameless before God.

OBSERVE

The city of Corinth was known for its immorality; in fact, the Greek verb translated *to Corinthianize* meant "to practice sexual immorality." Keep this in mind as you read the following passage from Paul's letter to the church at Corinth.

Leader: Read aloud 1 Corinthians 6:9-11. Have the group…
- *circle every occurrence of the pronoun* **you.**
- *underline the phrase* **do not be deceived.**

1 CORINTHIANS 6:9-11

9 Or do you not know that the unrighteous will not inherit the kingdom of God? Do not be deceived; neither fornicators, nor idolaters, nor adulterers, nor effeminate, nor homosexuals,

10 nor thieves, nor the covetous, nor drunkards, nor revilers, nor swindlers, will inherit the kingdom of God.

11 Such were some of you; but you were washed, but you were sanctified, but you were justified in the name of the Lord Jesus Christ and in the Spirit of our God.

INSIGHT

The definitions below explain some of the terms used in this passage that may be unfamiliar to you.

Fornicators—those who indulge in sexual immorality.

Idolaters—those who worship false gods.

Adulterers—those married persons who engage in sexual acts with those other than their mates.

Effeminate—effeminate by perversion. Deuteronomy 22:5 states, "Nor shall a man put on a woman's clothing; for whoever does these things is an abomination to the LORD your God."

Homosexuals—those men who indulge in sexual acts with other males.

Thieves—those who take what belongs to others.

Covetous—those who desire what others have.

(continued on page 83)

(continued from page 82)

Drunkards—those who abuse wine
and are habitually intoxicated.
Revilers—those who slander others
with their words with the intent to
destroy.
Swindlers—those who take unfair
advantage of others for their own
gain.

DISCUSS

• What deception did Paul warn his readers
about?

• According to verses 9 and 10, what is the
character or lifestyle of those who are not
going to inherit the kingdom of God?

INSIGHT

Paul described what happened to the Corinthians who became believers:

They were *washed* through the new birth experience, cleansed from their former sinful lifestyle.

They were *sanctified* through the indwelling of the Holy Spirit, setting them apart from the sinful society in which they lived to be consecrated to God for His purposes. The resulting behavioral pattern of obedience and holiness demonstrated a transformed life.

They were *justified,* declared righteous before God, and acquitted of every charge against them because of their faith in Jesus Christ as their Savior.

• What did you learn from verse 11 about the former lifestyle of some of the believers in Corinth?

• What changes had taken place in their lives, and what is the consequence of these changes?

OBSERVE

Leader: *Read 2 Corinthians 5:17.*

• *Have the group circle the words **anyone** and **he.***

DISCUSS

• Where is this person in relationship to Christ?

• What does that make this person?

• What events accompany this transformation?

• How does this compare with what you just learned in 1 Corinthians 6:9-11?

---

2 CORINTHIANS 5:17

Therefore if anyone is in Christ, he is a new creature; the old things passed away; behold, new things have come.

INSIGHT

The phrase *new creature* means we are a qualitatively new creation. In other words, we have new qualities. We now have the Holy Spirit of God dwelling within us to lead us, guide us, teach us, and empower us to do His will.

2 Corinthians 13:5

Test yourselves to see if you are in the faith; examine yourselves! Or do you not recognize this about yourselves, that Jesus Christ is in you—unless indeed you fail the test?

OBSERVE

The verses we just looked at reveal that the provision God has made for the believer's victory over sexual temptation is to be *in Christ*—to be washed, sanctified, and justified. We are new creatures with new qualities. But how can you be sure that this is true in your own life?

Leader: Read aloud 2 Corinthians 13:5.
  • *Have the group circle each occurrence of* **you** *and* **yourselves.**

DISCUSS

• Look at every place you circled *you* and *yourselves*. What did you learn from each one?

• Now let's do what this verse says. Let's test ourselves to see if we are in the faith.

Leader: Lead your group in a time of prayer, asking each man to examine himself to see if he is in the faith, if Jesus Christ is in him.

Your prayer might go something like this:

Father, we are pausing in our study
time this week to be obedient to the
truth we've learned in Your Word; we
desire to examine ourselves to see if
we are in the faith.

I am asking You through Your
Holy Spirit to reveal to me the truth
about my relationship with You. Is
Jesus Christ in my life or not?

Have I been washed, sanctified,
and justified? Have I been born
again? Am I a new creature in Your
sight? Or do the characteristics of the
unrighteous describe the pattern of
my life today?

Pause to allow the Spirit of God to bear
witness with your spirit as to whether or
not you are God's child. If God reveals that
you are not in the faith, then pray this
prayer:

God, I want to receive Jesus Christ
into my life by faith. I believe that
Jesus died on the cross for me so that

I might be forgiven of my sins. I confess my sins and desire to repent of my sinful ways. I ask You now to forgive me, cleanse me, and come into my heart.

If God reveals that you are in the faith, then thank Him that you are saved, that you are washed, sanctified, and justified. Rejoice in the knowledge that you are a new creature, that you are in Christ, that you have eternal life!

EPHESIANS 5:3-13

³ But immorality or any impurity or greed must not even be named among you, as is proper among saints;

⁴ and there must be no filthiness and silly talk, or coarse jesting, which are not fitting, but rather giving of thanks.

OBSERVE

Now let's look at some specific ways God instructs His children to deal with temptations.

Leader: Read aloud Ephesians 5:3-13 and have the group…
- *draw a cloud around every reference to **immorality**.*
- *underline every **command** or **instruction**.*

INSIGHT

A *saint* is a sanctified believer, one who is pure, holy, and blameless in heart and life. The word *saint* comes from the same root word in the Greek as the word *holy*. It means "to be set apart, consecrated to God."

DISCUSS

• What did you learn from marking *immorality*?

• What are the commands and instructions in this passage? What is God telling us as men that we should or should not do?

5 For this you know with certainty, that no immoral or impure person or covetous man, who is an idolater, has an inheritance in the kingdom of Christ and God.

6 Let no one deceive you with empty words, for because of these things the wrath of God comes upon the sons of disobedience.

7 Therefore do not be partakers with them;

8 for you were formerly darkness, but now you are Light in the Lord; walk as children of Light

9 (for the fruit of the Light consists in all goodness and righteousness and truth),

10 trying to learn what is pleasing to the Lord.

11 Do not participate in the unfruitful deeds of darkness, but instead even expose them;

12 for it is disgraceful even to speak of the things which are done by them in secret.

13 But all things become visible when they are exposed by the light, for everything that becomes visible is light.

• According to verses 5 and 6, what does God want us to know so we won't be deceived?

• According to this passage and what you read in 2 Corinthians, if immorality is your habitual lifestyle, what will happen to you?

• What parallels do you find between Ephesians 5:5-6 and 1 Corinthians 6:9-11?

PROVERBS 28:13

He who conceals his transgressions will not prosper, but he who confesses and forsakes them will find compassion.

OBSERVE

If you have committed some type of sexual immorality, what should you do?

Leader: *Read aloud Proverbs 28:13.*
  • *Have the group circle each occurrence of* **he** *and* **his.**

DISCUSS

• What did you learn from marking *he* and *his* in this verse?

• What should you do if you're guilty of a transgression? How will God respond?

INSIGHT

Covenant Eyes Internet Accountability software removes the secrecy of using the Internet. You choose accountability partners who are programmed in to every Web site you visit. This is not a filter. Rather, it provides direct accountability, cannot be erased or bypassed, and is dependable, inexpensive, and easy to use. You can sign up and download this unique Internet service program via e-mail. For more information visit www.covenanteyes.com or call toll free 877-479-1119.

1 JOHN 1:9

If we confess our sins, He is faithful and righteous to forgive us our sins and to cleanse us from all unrighteousness.

OBSERVE

Leader: Read aloud 1 John 1:9. Have the group do the following:

- *Circle each occurrence of **we, our,** and **us.***
- *Mark **He,** which refers to God, with a triangle:* △

INSIGHT

The word *confess* describes the action of specifically naming your sin and calling it what it is. In other words, confession involves saying the same thing about your sin that God says about it.

DISCUSS

- What did you learn from marking *we, our,* and *us?*

- What did you learn from marking the reference to God? What specifically does He do for us?

OBSERVE

Leader: Read aloud Galatians 5:16-25. Have the group do the following:

- *Draw a box around each reference to* **the Spirit.**
- *Circle the pronouns* **you, we,** *and* **us,** *which refer to* **believers.**
- *Mark each reference to* **the flesh** *with a slash, like this:* ╱

DISCUSS

- What did you learn from marking *you* in verses 16-18?

- According to verses 16-18, what two factions are in conflict in the believer's life?

GALATIANS 5:16-25

16 But I say, walk by the Spirit, and you will not carry out the desire of the flesh.

17 For the flesh sets its desire against the Spirit, and the Spirit against the flesh; for these are in opposition to one another, so that you may not do the things that you please.

18 But if you are led by the Spirit, you are not under the Law.

19 Now the deeds of the flesh are evident, which are: immorality, impurity, sensuality,

20 idolatry, sorcery, enmities, strife, jealousy, outbursts of anger, disputes, dissensions, factions,

21 envying, drunken-
ness, carousing, and
things like these, of
which I forewarn you,
just as I have fore-
warned you, that those
who practice such
things will not inherit
the kingdom of God.

22 But the fruit of the
Spirit is love, joy,
peace, patience, kind-
ness, goodness, faith-
fulness,

23 gentleness, self-
control; against such
things there is no law.

24 Now those who
belong to Christ Jesus
have crucified the flesh
with its passions and
desires.

25 If we live by the
Spirit, let us also walk
by the Spirit.

• What did you learn from marking *the
flesh* and *you* in verses 19-21?

• According to verses 22-23, how do you
know if you are walking in the Spirit?

• What did you learn from marking *the
flesh* and *the Spirit* in verses 24-25?

• According to this passage, what must you
do to have victory over your sexual
desires, temptations, and passions?

OBSERVE

Leader: Read aloud Philippians 4:8. Have the group:

- *Circle the words* **brethren** *and* **your,** *which refer to* **believers.**

DISCUSS

- What did you learn from marking the references to believers?

- According to God's instruction in this passage, what can we do to ensure victory over our temptations and desires?

- What standard does this passage set for the believer?

- What sort of practical impact would this have on the everyday life of a Christian man?

- Based on everything you've learned up to this point, how would continuously "dwell[ing] on these things" help you abstain from sexual immorality?

PHILIPPIANS 4:8

Finally, brethren, whatever is true, whatever is honorable, whatever is right, whatever is pure, whatever is lovely, whatever is of good repute, if there is any excellence and if anything worthy of praise, dwell on these things.

PSALM 119:9-11

9 How can a young man keep his way pure? By keeping it according to Your word.

10 With all my heart I have sought You; do not let me wander from Your commandments.

11 Your word I have treasured in my heart, that I may not sin against You.

2 PETER 1:3-4

3 Seeing that His divine power has granted to us everything pertaining to life and godliness, through the true knowledge of Him who called us by His own glory and excellence.

OBSERVE

Leader: Read aloud Psalm 119:9-11.

- *Have the group circle every reference to* **the young man,** *including the pronouns* **my, I,** *and* **me.**

DISCUSS

- What did you learn from marking the references to the young man? What is he seeking to do?

- How could he achieve his objective?

- According to this passage, what actions can you take to abstain from sexual immorality?

OBSERVE

Leader: Read aloud 2 Peter 1:3-4. Have the group...

- *circle every reference to* **the believers,** *indicated by the pronouns* **us** *and* **you.**
- *underline each occurrence of the word* **granted.**

DISCUSS

• What did you learn from marking the references to believers in these verses?

• What has the believer escaped?

• How would knowing this help you abstain from sexual immorality?

OBSERVE

Leader: Read aloud James 4:7-8a.
  • *Have the group number each of **the instructions.***

DISCUSS

• The Bible teaches us that we are at war with the devil. According to this passage, what three things are we to do when temptation comes?

• What will be the results of our obedience?

4 For by these He has granted to us His precious and magnificent promises, so that by them you may become partakers of the divine nature, having escaped the corruption that is in the world by lust.

JAMES 4:7-8A

7 Submit therefore to God. Resist the devil and he will flee from you.

8 Draw near to God and He will draw near to you.

WRAP IT UP

You have been granted everything pertaining to life and godliness. You have been granted God's precious and magnificent promises so that by them you may become a partaker of the divine nature.

Though you formerly indulged in the desires of the flesh and of the mind, you are now a new creature in Christ. You can choose to walk by the Spirit and no longer carry out the desires of your flesh.

However, you must observe God's commandments and not forsake His teachings. His Word guides you when you walk, watches over you when you sleep, talks to you when you are awake, reproves you when you are wrong, and keeps you from the adulteress.

Submit to God. Resist the devil and he will flee from you. Make no provision for the flesh. Avoid anything that might lead to sexual promiscuity and sensuality, including allowing your thoughts or eyes to linger on inappropriate images. Be careful what you watch, what you read, what you listen to, where you go, what you say, and who you are alone with.

If you have been guilty of gazing at women, fantasizing about sexual acts with someone, or dreaming about adulterous affairs, confess it as sin and draw near to God through the study of His Word.

If you've seen or read something you shouldn't have, said something that was sensual or flirtatious, or put yourself in a potentially tempting position, confess your sin, forsake it, and commit never to do it again. Take those thoughts captive and think on those things that are honorable, right, pure, lovely, of good repute, excellent, and worthy of praise.

Sexual sin violates your own body, violates the other person, and violates her present or future husband. But most importantly, sexual sin violates your relationship with God. If you try to conceal it, you will not prosper or get away with it. If you confess it and turn from it, you will receive God's compassion and forgiveness.

He has done His part. Will you do yours? Will you live a pure, holy, blameless life that is pleasing to Him? This is the will of God for your life: your sanctification. He desires that you abstain from sexual immorality, controlling your thoughts, desires, and passions.

FOR FURTHER READING

Every Man's Battle: Winning the War on Sexual Temptation by
Stephen Arterburn and Fred Stoeker with Mike Yorkey.
Colorado Springs: WaterBrook, 2000.

*Beneath the Surface: Steering Clear of the Dangers That Could
Leave You Shipwrecked* by Bob Reccord. Nashville: Broad-
man & Holman, 2002.

The Truth About Sex by Kay Arthur. Colorado Springs: Water-
Brook, 2005.

40 MINUTE BIBLE STUDIES

No-Homework
That Help You

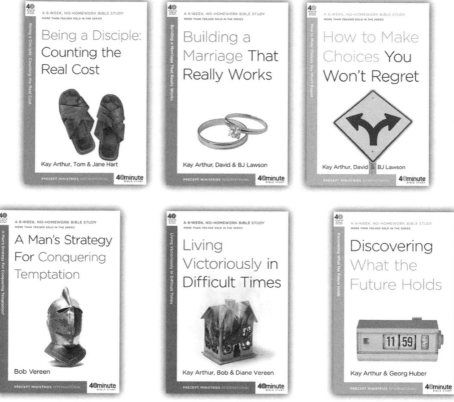

A 6-WEEK, NO-HOMEWORK BIBLE STUDY
MORE THAN 700,000 SOLD IN THE SERIES

Being a Disciple:
Counting the
Real Cost

Kay Arthur, Tom & Jane Hart

A 6-WEEK, NO-HOMEWORK BIBLE STUDY
MORE THAN 700,000 SOLD IN THE SERIES

Building a
Marriage That
Really Works

Kay Arthur, David & BJ Lawson

A 6-WEEK, NO-HOMEWORK BIBLE STUDY
MORE THAN 700,000 SOLD IN THE SERIES

How to Make
Choices You
Won't Regret

Kay Arthur, David & BJ Lawson

A 6-WEEK, NO-HOMEWORK BIBLE STUDY
MORE THAN 700,000 SOLD IN THE SERIES

A Man's Strategy
For Conquering
Temptation

Bob Vereen

A 6-WEEK, NO-HOMEWORK BIBLE STUDY
MORE THAN 700,000 SOLD IN THE SERIES

Living
Victoriously in
Difficult Times

Kay Arthur, Bob & Diane Vereen

A 6-WEEK, NO-HOMEWORK BIBLE STUDY
MORE THAN 700,000 SOLD IN THE SERIES

Discovering
What the
Future Holds

Kay Arthur & Georg Huber

A 6-WEEK, NO-HOMEWORK BIBLE STUDY
MORE THAN 700,000 SOLD IN THE SERIES

Key Principles
of Biblical
Fasting

Kay Arthur & Pete De Lacy

A 6-WEEK, NO-HOMEWORK BIBLE STUDY
MORE THAN 700,000 SOLD IN THE SERIES

Forgiveness:
Breaking the
Power of the Past

Kay Arthur, David & BJ Lawson

Bible Studies
Discover Truth For Yourself

A 6-WEEK, NO-HOMEWORK BIBLE STUDY
MORE THAN 700,000 SOLD IN THE SERIES

How Do You Know God's Your Father?
Kay Arthur, David & BJ Lawson

How Do You Walk the Walk You Talk?
Kay Arthur

Money and Possessions: The Quest for Contentment
Kay Arthur & David Arthur

The Essentials of Effective Prayer
Kay Arthur, David & BJ Lawson

Having a Real Relationship with God
Kay Arthur

Rising to the Call of Leadership
Kay Arthur, David & BJ Lawson

What Does the Bible Say About Sex?
Kay Arthur, David & BJ Lawson

Living a Life of True Worship
Kay Arthur, Bob & Diane Vereen

Another powerful study series from beloved Bible teacher

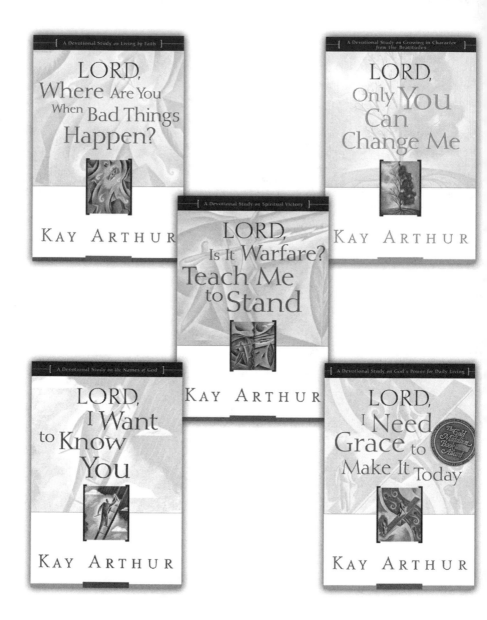

{ A Devotional Study on Living by Faith }

LORD,
Where Are You When Bad Things Happen?

KAY ARTHUR

{ A Devotional Study on Growing in Character from the Beatitudes }

LORD,
Only You Can Change Me

KAY ARTHUR

{ A Devotional Study on Spiritual Victory }

LORD,
Is It Warfare?
Teach Me to Stand

KAY ARTHUR

{ A Devotional Study on the Names of God }

LORD,
I Want to Know You

KAY ARTHUR

{ A Devotional Study on God's Power for Daily Living }

LORD,
I Need Grace to Make It Today

The Gold Medallion Book Award

KAY ARTHUR

KAY ARTHUR

The Lord series provides insightful, warm-hearted Bible studies designed to meet you where you are —and help you discover God's answers to your deepest needs.

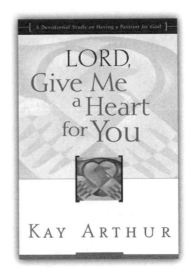

ALSO AVAILABLE:
One-year devotionals to draw you closer to the heart of God.

BOB VEREEN serves as an ambassador-at-large for Precept Ministries International, along with his wife, Diane. The couple speak at conferences around the world and oversee a number of Precept's international offices. They both travel the globe teaching people how to study the Bible inductively as well as mentoring and training national leadership. They have been on staff since 1991, following sixteen years of prior involvement with Precept Ministries International. Bob was a contributor to *The New Inductive Study Bible* and has written for the New Inductive Study Series and the 40-Minute Bible Studies series.

PRECEPT MINISTRIES INTERNATIONAL, founded in 1970 by Jack and Kay Arthur, has a worldwide outreach that establishes children, teens, and adults in God's Word. In addition to inductive study training workshops and thousands of small-group studies across America, PMI reaches nearly 150 countries with inductive Bible studies translated into nearly 70 languages, teaching people to discover Truth for themselves.

Contact Precept Ministries International for more information about inductive Bible studies in your area.

Precept Ministries International
P.O. Box 182218
Chattanooga, TN 37422-7218
800-763-8280
www.precept.org